Adolescence, Adulthood, and Ambivalence: Poetry and Self-Reflectivity

Jessica Hattemer

BookLeaf
Publishing

India | USA | UK

Presentation by *BookLeaf Publishing*

Web: www.bookleafpub.com

E-mail: info@bookleafpub.com

ISBN: 9789363306561

First edition 2024

In loving memory of my grandfather, Peapaw. I love you so much. I am so blessed you came to my first graduation since I missed my high school graduation due to Covid in 2020. Graduating with my bachelor's degree and seeing you in the stands cheering for me will always be a core memory. I'll cherish every moment we spent and I'll keep shining bright in my academics.

Foreign Dreams

Cherry blossoms, wooden stalks.
Golden sunlit, warming walks.

In your mind, in a trance.
Cranes nearby, cry and dance.

Is this real? Is this fake?
There's koi fish swimming, in the lake.

School bells ring, loud and clear.
The trance you're in, its end is near.

Mental escape, to a foreign land.
It kicks you out, in reprimand.

The stress of reality pulls you back.
Your Japanese getaway quickly turns black.

Don't wander off, like a wayward soul.
The future's bright, with a rewarding goal.

You must work hard, and win this fight.
As your mental escape is in your sight.

No hallucinations, prepared you for this.

The determination, wasn't an accomplice.

You steered your focus, to make things new.
From a glum black aura to a shimmering blue.

Dreams can harvest, newfound passions.
Like making sushi, from healthy rations.

To learn a language, and be fluent.
For speaking proper, and congruent.

Koi fish here, lily pads there.
Clouds as intricate, as sculpted ware.

Study hard and learn, how to soar.
Reach out your hand, and discover more.

You Are Loved

Why are we just fighting all the time?

For an endless war of emotional damage.

Can't we live in peace for just a little while?

Peace is nothing but an acronym for successful failures.

Can everyone silence themselves before damaging those they wish to never hurt in the first place?

The chilling remnants of societal imbalances and empty promises are forming what we call "stability," yet we choose to act upon our emotions irrationally.

Is the confinement to basic standards and social trends how we should live our lives to avoid possible harassment?

The human mind's capability to escape the pain of public imagery is by expressing raw and unfiltered emotions through different mediums.

As these questions are being answered in your head, in my head, the biggest question remains: are we as humans truly capable of exerting love with means to support others? Whether it's familial, romantic, or platonic love, can people understand how their words hurt someone if they deny love in a certain way?

These inner dialogues cancel out any positive outlook on what love could be or how it can be painted. No one is undeserving of love; we all fall short of the glory of God and whatever religion/denomination we choose to belong to. Deep affection, slow to anger, tender upbringing. Calm. Complicated. Difficult. Useless. Serene.

Love can be anything you want, but the greatest love of all is learning how to love yourself before putting yourself down in the gutter. Building self-compassion, lowering stress, and building higher resilience are three key components of self-love. Staying mentally aligned with the goals you have is how you develop a willingness to take risks (the good kind of course), to create empathy in the acceptance of strengths and weaknesses, and to set boundaries of the "yes" or "no" we face in reality.

You are not alone. Sometimes seeking external validation and approval excessively or comparing oneself unfavorably to others is either a habit or a subconscious pattern, but you can break through it. Loving yourself is hard and thinking that you deserve it or don't deserve it is a self-sabotage for yourself. I challenge you to remind yourself that embracing who you are is going to imprint positivity into the one life you have to live. Build new habits, love yourself, and discover what love is to you. Food, drinks, a gas station, a lake, a library, a novelty item, your bedroom, the aquarium, with people, etc.

You are worthy of love.

Love is complicated,
It has many roots.
Joy is anticipated,
It bears many fruits.

While self-love tests your
Ability to find oneself.
Self-compassion allows
You to forgive yourself.

We seek validation,
To feel acceptance.
Sadly the causation,
Causes reflectance.

Don't eat the wrong fruits
From the wrong tree.
Find your peace within,
To set your mind free.

Positivity annihilated,
Self-sabotaging your mind.
Perfectionism obliterated,
Grow compassion and be kind.

The time is now,
To plant your seeds of love.
Remember to embrace yourself,
As the sun shines from above.

Trauma Drama Llamas

Trauma. The trigger to depressive episodes. The link that carries us to a solidarity of elusive thoughts of happy wishings. Teenagers and adults alike have triggering memories of traumatic events in their lives. These events create delayed responses with fatigue, fear of recurrence, anxiety-focused flashbacks, and depression. The stressors created by these distressing moments in our lives inflict fear into ourselves to live warily of the "what-ifs". Some of the core memories in our lives resonate with those traumas in either good or bad responses.

When it comes to trauma, we often shut down or unload it to people in a fairly dark and humorous way. The times that we look to block these moments is when it's delving deep into the past of books we wished to keep closed. The point is, you aren't going to fall. You can bounce back stronger than you ever thought you could. Through time.
You are not alone. The trauma you have experienced is not something you should keep inside yourself; instead, journal it out. A journal is a best friend, a safe space to write anything

down. Isolation is NOT the way, rather, surround yourself with others and face it. It's natural to feel depleted of hope but don't lose your grip!

I've experienced so much in my life, but I've found my peace of mind, which is God. For some, it can be through yoga and meditation, for others coping with trauma, it can be attending therapy and support groups that conduct craft activities together. There are various methodologies to rejuvenate yourself from the wearied taxation trauma has on your mind. There's no better feeling than to face your trauma and convert it into fueling passion to conquer your fears and reach new heights. Find your healthy medium, create new passions, and don't let your trauma become drama, be happy like a llama.

Llamas are fluffy and happy animals that are currently used as therapy animals in some regions. Whenever you feel down, think of a happy llama.

Don't get caught in trauma drama, instead think of happy llamas!

Insomnia: 12:30 p.m. - 2:40 a.m.

I've been up restlessly scrolling through the internet. Surely the technology and the darkness will subdue the mind, right? Wrong. Everyone knows that the overwhelming usage of technology before rest is damaging in many ways. Especially with your eyes in the dark, it strains them. When you stare at the small screen with no interest in recollecting what was searched during this time, you wonder. Through the reels or posts, it's an endless scrolling battle, an addicting one. Some that are most popular are the ones you might save into your favorites folder or just like the post to "hopefully remember it for later to share with the friend who often browses over your sent posts." Moreover, I've realized in my endless scrolling that apps can be quite different from each other.

For example, Instagram has a great demographic and has content for all ages, mainly suitable for those 15-40 (in my opinion). Puppies that run with floppy ears are almost as animatic as Dumbo's giant ears. Or maybe the reel with the toddler who spoke its first word but learned how

to curse from a late 1980s RomCom series on
television. Sometimes it's a mixture of the
political divisions we face through uncovered
surface tension that'll soon eradicate the
individuals who saw right through the
government. All covered up as a murder mystery
or a fantastical suicide extravaganza. Maybe the
fossils we see and structures in the islands are of
what's to come in the unforeseeable future that's
breaking apart in front of us. The best of all is
the unexplainably hilarious memes that we have
yet to truly disseminate for the true purpose they
serve, yet they grow so popular and die so
quickly.

Facebook is a mix of reality television shows,
fishing trips with compilations of the biggest
catches, expecting parents and live deliveries for
the world to see for educational purposes,
gender reveals, animal videos (the most
popular), and of course the comedians and how
their borderline racist/activist
feminist/controversialist, etc. comment that
arguably strikes an internet feud. This platform
is for all ages but yet again I don't find myself
going on there to communicate with others or
post, I just wander, endlessly until I've had my
fill for the time being. I also get too indulged in
the marketplace feature and I laugh at some of

the products listed. I wish I bought that antique sign from that gas station.

Why do we get so attached? I don't understand it but, from my brain-twisting analogy, I've grown accustomed to doing this; scrolling with no thoughts behind my eyes as they droop so heavily. My mind goes blank and all the white noise static I hear grows louder. The time goes out the window; before I knew it, 12:30 a.m. is now 2:56 a.m. because of the constant scrolling. Technology is a huge cause of the problem, but sometimes I put the phone down. Then that opens the door to an entirely new way of thinking. Recollecting the day that transpired, all the good, bad, and the ugly. Where did it all go wrong, or why do I think things went wrong today? It was pretty simple. Why did my left foot go numb at 3:29 p.m. at the coffee shop in anticipation of cooling down the burn of the Hot Funyons I just consumed in my car? Why do I get anxious when I think of a relationship because of my past traumas I have yet to overcome and be at peace with? Can I truly expect to be successful in three years if the world is inevitably meeting its end as the Bible laid it out? Are we in the end times? Can I ever have the dreams of having children or will I die of the knowingness that life was nothing but a

test to be a faithful servant? Do people truly
know that giants existed and roamed the Earth
so by covering this up with theoretical jargon,
are we accepting of what's happened and what'll
be uncovered? The list of random headspace
thoughts is surging.

We often get lost in our minds.

Mind over matter.
Matter over mind.
The world surrounds us,
In a toxic bind.

Theory is factual.
Facts are theories.
Time is short as
We seek inquiries.

Can we find the way?
The world will never know.
Our truth is found in
Heavy leveled snow.

Dreams. What Are They?

Dreams. What are they? Are they something but a mere figment in your mind? Are they depictions of what life would look like in different circumstances? Or maybe they're meant to be a temporary source of dopamine to where you feel pleasurable shocks of euphoria? Dreams can be anything: a dream job with a sports car, a getaway, or all the valuables you crave right at your fingertips. Dreams can be impractical: a Pegasus named Daffodil transporting you to the castle in the cloud, a fantasy where you're the main trope of the saga or even a place where you had time-manipulating powers to get everything you ever wanted. Dreams can be memories. Memories of a bittersweet time building puzzles with your grandfather when he had bursts of life; or the time you shot strawberry milk out of your nose on pizza Fridays in high school.

Dreams have the power of imagination and creativity to fuel those thoughts, but what about those who can't dream? They are unable to fathom their abilities to think of either life or beauty and resort to succumbing to self-harm.

Where there's no such thing as "a happy ending"
because fairytales are deceiving. Some people
can't find dreams and in the pit of their guts,
they wallow in the misery of past mistakes,
begging their sources of comfort to alleviate the
pain of yesterday. With all that in fruition,
dreams to them are a fallacy.

Inner thoughts and self-reflection. A person who
lacks the creative mind finds it as a moment of
self-reflection. 'How can one person dream and
believe such idiocy? Ludicrous grimy thoughts.
Wretched.' What often becomes of those
individuals is thinking outside the box of their
isolation. Maybe all this time they dared to
dream. As a teenager undergoing puberty, I felt
all these things. As a young adult, I still grasp
onto my dreams. To travel to Japan; to be a
successful businesswoman, and to live
comfortably with my future children —
whenever that time would come. As you think
over and over about the spiraling events of both
life and misfortune, reality hits you like a bomb,
detonating all the doubts in your mind.

Dreams. They produce vitality and nourishment
to feed your inner child. The one who innocently
dreamed about the job they wished to reach; like
a star in the sky. You can't grasp that star, but

you wish and dream about the day you can
become an astronaut and fly amongst them.
Twinkling sprinkles of cosmic glitter littered
over a black canvas, with globs of color from
planets, to comets, and meteors. No one can
define who you are and what your purpose
should be in life. The potential you have to make
the most of what's given to you displays the
truth that, "a dream is a wish your heart makes."
Find your passions to be innovative, dream
about the goals you wish to seek, and watch as
your reality forms not only with your two hands
but with the doors that God lays in front of you.

Dreams are unique,
In the palm of your hand.
They transport you off,
To a faraway land.

Glimmering waters of
Silver and blue.
The tidal waves curl
And change their hue.

You're in a field now,
With galloping elks.
It's trail leads you back,
To the lightning whelks.

Seashells found
And seashells lost.
Dreams are endless,
Like a winter frost.

Road Trips

Sounds of gravel chunks,
Hit the car underneath.
Wind whirling quickly,
From the elevation beneath.

Warblers and songbirds,
Sing up from the pines.
Cumulus and orographic,
Clouds form designs.

Constant brake checks,
With sounds of screeching.
Rain clouds forming,
As the rain starts breaching.

Soft and heavy rainfall,
Hit the glass indifferently.
It's the mediocre pace of decent,
Went from loud to silently.

The sun breaks through,
And the sun hits my leg.
Thoughts of home cry,
And my brain starts to beg.

"Go home, don't travel,
You don't need to explore."
Yet my heart knows differently,
As it earnestly implores.

"Don't get lost in your mind,
Live and break free."
Silencing my thoughts,
I break from conformity.

Life is short and wild,
There's so much to see.
I'm not confined to time,
To haste my commodity.

Time is of the essence,
As the road grows green.
Trees surrounding the car,
The atmosphere is so serene.

Traveling is exciting,
Whether it's short or long.
The memories you make,
Will last all lifelong.

Political Division, Divine Provision.

Whether it's nationwide, or specifically in my home country of the United States of America, there is a political division. The amendment to have free speech and expression of a multitude of beliefs seems to have been shaken off the Constitution like an Etch A Sketch. From controversial approaches to proclamatory indifferences, we the people have lost what it means to stand in unity.

Wherever you stand, in whichever boundary you've built your walls and property on, there are pros and cons of what people will think of you. The will to hold onto what you believe or the guilt to succumb to the pure hatred and benevolence of your oppressors will grasp both of your hands. In the prejudice of what people think is right from wrong shouldn't make you falter.

When you lose your momentum and purpose to keep driving forward in what you believe, it's only going to cause you more mental struggles and backlash from both sides, pro-this or against that, republican/conservative or democratic/liberal. The world will revolve with or without your opinion being heard, whether you like it or not.

Inevitably we are going to fall into the wrong hands, into the treacherous walk on a tightrope over the well-lit furnace by congressional bigshots and legislative snobs. If this becomes a poised threat, you must stand strong for what you believe, in spirituality, faith, political and governed beliefs, and especially for what will be for the betterment of your familial connections.

You have divine provisions to discern truth from fallacy. The end times to find your foundation are approaching rapidly at an unforeseeable rate. Stand firm in what you believe and guard it with diligence and humbleness. Retract animosity toward your neighbors and walk in the path of truth and acceptance. We as a nation are falling, and the world is alongside us falling quickly too. It's up to us to collectively raise our voices and protect each other before we all get pummeled by the giant, egotistical political bigots. Fight the good fight, not the wrong one.

Creatively Unique

Mental health is a serious issue; one that I've struggled with throughout my entire adolescence. The way that my life pivoted in the most unimaginable ways still baffles me. I used to have the most creative mindset as a young child and pre-teen and then as a teenager, it all dissipated. When you grow, your mind changes, and so does your body. What I've concluded is that from the amount of trauma, mental health problems, stress, anxiety, and depression that I've faced, I found most of my creative mediums and forms of expression through these hard times.

Many societal impacts influence the human mind and the way that we perceive information. Whether it's from a creative influencer that rises to the top in popularity and charisma, or it's from how incredibly ridiculous something sounds, we find ourselves being drawn to it. A popular example in the modern day is Taylor Swift. You see Swift everywhere and people are constantly drawn to her style, her music, and to create designs that resonate with her persona through cake, clothing, knitted products, etc.

In our lives, we have so many reasons for pain and suffering but yet we turn that into something unique; to what we perceive it as. Maybe in honor of a family pet passing, you create a wreath with its favorite toys and trinkets and hang it up around Christmas time so they still are involved. Maybe you find that you bombed your latest test and instead of getting too whirled into the depressive cyclone, you drain out the negativity by roller skating down the neighborhood blasting your favorite tunes. Negativity converted into creativity is a strong source of both excitement and the unlimited potential to discover more about yourself every day.

I challenge you, whenever you're down and feel depleted and defeated, create something new. A song, a dance, a drawing, a knitted/crocheted product, a baked good, etc. Use your negativity to fuel creativity and positivity. Think of your comforts and strive to be more than just restricted to your emotions. You aren't conformed to being alone in your room. There's a whole world of imagination and creativity to explore!

For me, I found my passion for writing when I was depressed at a young age. My family has always taken pride in its academics and the means to be a professional. For my mom, it was photography and going to the beach to collect shells. For my dad, it was writing screenplays and watching something new on the television. For my older brother, he was playing sports or getting out and being active, exploring the town. For my younger brother, it was culinary arts and learning how to fly planes through simulations to become a pilot one day.

You are not confined or limited to options on the way you should live your life. Remember to think outside the box, become a stronger person, and think positively with a creative outlook on life!

Is the Grass Greener?

I'm baffled by the depictions
Of my mind barricaded shut.
No screams can lace this
Bitter taste in my throat.

Crying is for children,
An avoidable weakness.
Is the grass greener on the other side,
Or have I just gone blank?

Green grass, blue skies.
One laughs, and the other cries.

Smiling is healthy,
The brain needs fuel.
Gloom excretes joy,
In a compelling duel.

Am I ready for life?
The challenges that lie ahead?
Or am I willfully drowning,
With water over my head?

Once a deprived teen,
Always depressed.
No, the tables have turned,
These feelings are repressed.

Fighting back for me,
I gasp aloud for air.
The scars of pain,
Knock me out of my chair.

Life is more than death,
It's more than sadness.
The daydreams I have,
Are of pure madness.

Faith, hope, and grace,
My foundation to wean,

Away from the drought,
To the grass that's green.

You have the strength to overcome every trial
and tribulation that you face. Only you can
decide what you do to get out of that situation.
You are wonderfully and fearfully made, choose
your path in the way that is right, true, and just
to the person you hope to become.

Pubescent Thoughts in Adolescence

This acne is the size of a crater on the moon. Bright and visible, it glistens in bodily oils like greasy fries in a fast-food chain. My legs are like a Sasquatch, I have thick, dark brown locks. I look at the other girls, the white swans in the pond. They sparkle and radiate while I'm the ugly duckling, gray in color, an eyesore. How can I be the swan and showcase a beauty that seems so foreign? I'm met with solitude as I am the needle in the haystack. How can I find inner beauty if my gray color reflects my feelings of self-love? Will I ever be a swan, one that's graceful and beautiful? Or will I stay smelling rancid like rotting trash at a five-star hotel, waiting to be taken to the dump?

Tulips

Why are tulips red? How do they get their hue?

Do they kiss the blood good morning on a sunny
afternoon?

Water slips through its petals, falling into soiled
ground

Where love is planted in, but the grass grows
over strong.

Can the tulips walk on solid ground and find my
beating heart?

Will they match the echo of my rib cage that is
being strung?

My arteries are being played like a harp in an
orchestra,

So where can I find the tulips, where can they be
found?

They play this song of happiness, it sounds so
unreal,

Tulips come from meadows filled with
gargantuan blue seals.

Are tulips leading congregation among the
people of the courtroom?

Do they know that if they win their battle, they
won't ever bloom?

These flowers are a mystery, they are red for a
reason.

Filled with love, laughter, and life, they laugh in
the breeze.

Why are tulips red? How do they get their hue?

Do they kiss the blood good morning on a sunny
afternoon?

Laughter is the Best Medicine

Ever heard of laughter being the best medicine? Well, in this case, it most certainly is. Laughter is a common reaction when something is amusing or when we have an excessive amount of joy. This can also be known as an endorphin rush which can give an overwhelming happiness. Laughter can formulate a boost of serotonin naturally raise levels of self-esteem and avoid emotional blockages. The ways of feeling true laughter can be broken down through what laughter is, the effects and benefits of laughter, and the examples of how it can be impactful.

Laughter is an emotion that results from something humorous and can be contagious. It is a pervasive human behavior that most frequently happens in social activities. This is something that we as humans do as a response to lighten the environment or to show others that there is enjoyment in the present activity or conversation. When there is excitement during a hormonal phase of our lives, it can be perceived

in different ways to which we find unassuming
or rude.

A lot of people in their adulthood forget that
laughter is something that should be a daily
habit. I know, as humorous as that may sound,
it's incredibly healthy for you. In Proverbs
17:22, it says in the verse, 'a merry heart does
good like medicine, but a broken spirit dries the
bones.' Laughter is complex and a
health-inducing phenomenon that strengthens or
breaks relationships in whichever context it is
used in. In life, we experience too much hurt to
not have enlightening periods of excitement and
joy to alleviate that pain. Find what makes you
happy and continue to be the best that you can
be!

Stop Signs and Society

Societal influences creep the sidewalks in mannerisms left noticeable but slightly unnoticeable. Maybe it's a sticker on the back of a stop sign, but what does it mean? What organizational ties does it have that we can't coherently decipher? It doesn't seem to be threatening since it's placed there, but what's the true meaning behind it? Masonry? Witchcraft? Gang-affiliated insignia? Or maybe it's a restaurant or a famously known brand. These are meant to give us an idea of what types of people are nearby in the area. Positive or negative, we all coexist in a juxtaposed manner. Black and white or white and black. Now, for my personal beliefs vandalism isn't a respectable thing to do, but for others, it's a sweet release from inner conflicts. A safe space where the mind runs wild to convey a message only that particular person or maybe a group, can decipher well enough.

You're probably wondering why a stop sign with stickers is something to write about, but when you think of it, you can write about anything. The weeds growing in the sidewalk cracks of a church whose pastor got charged with wiring funding from the tithes offering. Maybe you write about the puddle at the end of the driveway with microorganisms that wriggle around helplessly with the water bugs walking over them. Better yet, how about the bird that sings songs as beautifully as the spindle weaves a blanket for a newborn baby whose name reminds you of a soft winter fire? Anything is possible with the mind of creativity but also the knowingness of the world we live in. Yet, with intricate beauty lies the imperfection of human nature and its desire to pierce the silence. Silence of ordinary lifestyles ruptured with the sounds of war and the pursuit of self-defense. A stop sign with stickers won't save you from a bullet to the head but the self-awareness to protect yourself at any given moment could. In a society where life is tampered with, how will it meet its end? Can the way we live truly make a difference in a society built similarly to a hazardous minefield? As baffling as it may be, we take these moments for granted as they pass by quicker than the wind in a Category 5 hurricane.

I'm no historian or high-status ranked official who knows about the small but mighty town that I live in, but it's gotten...interesting.

Societal influences creep up,
The questions I have form.
People dress in different clothing,
Where questions in my head swarm.

Are they going to lunge?
Will they plan an attack?
Are they normal civilians,
Who wishes to fall back?

There are words I don't know,
All these phrases are confusing.
The people who use them,
Take a constant brain bruising.

Sounding rather sophisticated,
For a low-quality result.
I stand there baffled,
Spectating the insult.

Although I'm a bystander,
This civilization is doomed.
I can't tell if I'm right,
Or if I wrongly assumed.

Who's To Know?

What are the concepts that makeup who we are as people? In such a short time, I've come to realize that my true potential lies where my interests are uprooted. Each sprout of inspiration grows into a garden of interest; inevitably each interest is dug up when it's ready to be used. In my adolescent years, I never understood what I was meant to do or what life was about. Amid the confusion, there were questions I always asked myself. What's so fancy about working a 9-5 behind the counter answering aggravated middle-aged constituents who complain about their issues? If my parents found ways beyond an eight-hour shift job, then why can't I do something different?

For some reason, I've pondered on what exactly humans were created to do if there's nothing but stress and aggravation. Deep down, some things make us different and stand out from the rest. These things are what draw me closer to the questions that are left unanswered, rhetorical statements.

It's a vague, open-ended question with no right or wrong answers. This is a million-dollar question that won't have a certain answer. You won't win the lottery if you formulate an answer on the top of your head and you won't go bankrupt for taking your time. This is something that I find myself asking not only myself but others. The input of others, from what I've learned gradually, is an intelligent way to learn more about your values.

As children, our chemical makeup is different than the average adult's. They think meticulously, ask open-ended questions, and find ways to think outside the box toward discovering new things. It was always a phenomenon to me seeing how a child can pinpoint details an adult can't and find wondrous ways to stir the pot. They stir mischief and childlike antics but also learn from the mistakes made to become the person they're meant to be. As a child, I was the one to ask questions and be bratty when things didn't go routine. I found it difficult to understand how others communicated what I wanted properly.

What are we meant to be and what do we wish to seek out?

Life is so short and yet we find ways to feel
excited about anything and everything. I hope
that by finding who you are, and how your
potential is limitless, you can challenge yourself
to find the good in the confusing transitions.

Rain

Humidity is horrid, drenching in sweat in under five minutes. The way the ultraviolet rays kiss my slightly tanned skin and start to turn in color imitates the first kiss of a young couple as their faces turn red. It is late August; the summer has ended, and fall is approaching. Thunder in the distance comes, it sounds like a lion's roar. The all-familiar scent rolls into my nostrils. I can smell the rain. The distinctive scent it gives off from the pavement of the road scratches an itch in my head that bewilders my senses. The swift breeze that picks up right before the storm hits is followed by the light mist of droplets. The branches bend in unison, like a yoga instructor with their class. Winds start picking up and the banging on the glass increases. I'm met now with a raging storm, the lightning sounding like the millions of clapping people in a crowd. Although it is loud, the comfort of my couch in the living room makes it peaceful. The frogs are croaking a song of harmony, and the wilderness takes in the cool breeze that escaped the hand of humidity. A blissful reminder that Mother Nature is a masterpiece in this now gloomy storm. The blades of grass are thanking the clouds as the tsunami-like downpour on the plants increases. I can see the sawgrass bend harshly and the trees swaying in the wind. A mouthful of tuna fish and a relaxed mind have led me to take in this phenomenon. One that people take for granted, is the power of rain.

Heartbreak

Amid heartbreak, your body undergoes not only psychological warfare but a crisis in which your emotions don't align. It's a jumble of hindrances that prohibit you from moving forward with ease and a stable mindset. From my personal experience, I found myself lost in the shadows of sorrow and, in a way, guilt. When the decision is made to separate from what you thought a long-term relationship would be, you feel torn and incredibly feeble in new situations. The reality of a break-up and losing your "first love" is something irreplaceable that will take time to heal. The moment that happens, you can let yourself grieve properly

When you feel lost and uncertain about how to feel and how to relieve yourself of this agony, you take a moment to reflect. You take a moment to heal the wound that was imprinted on your heart and to alleviate the heavy weight on your shoulders. In the healing process, it takes time to self-reflect on your values, virtues, and what makes you so unique from others. I find that some would find themselves amazed at how many small tidbits of their personality have been suppressed in a relationship. Others may feel obligated to feel the way they do at that moment for years to come. I find it incredibly difficult to let go of these emotions even now. The love that I still have will forever blaze in my heart but in my mind, I've let go of what that unforeseeable future could've been.

Relationships, in my opinion, were meant to be where two are made as one and hold God in the center of their lives. Equally yoked, equally understanding each other, and always there to lend a hand where it was deemed necessary. I thought that in my first long-term relationship, I had it all aligned. In being the person that I was, I've come to realize that I was out of place in more ways than one. For example, if a young couple in their early 20s comes together and finds a rhythm that matches their pitches, they're bound to make harmonious melodies. Now, if a young couple in their early teenage years came together and were still finding their tunes and learning new chords, the song they sing together comes out with hiccups and rough edges. Not all relationships that start from a young age are bound for disaster or an inevitable separation. Some of these relationships learn new notes, find the right keys, and make songs that sound smooth as butter. It all takes time, patience, and a willingness to learn from each other.

Being torn in a relationship was one of the most difficult things I had dealt with, especially when it came to being upfront about emotions or asking for simple things. I'm not the most effective communicator, but I tend to get my message across by beating around the bush. Not only did this lead to arguments as pointless as a circle, but it also led to the dishonesty of holding conversations that aligned with greater problems. It's okay to feel upset or uncomfortable about certain topics when you first date someone, but after some time, these topics should be easier to discuss.

What does this all mean? Why is there an analogy about music and the way that it aligns with another individual? I mention this because, in the psychological aspect of music and heartbreak, you can find yourself playing at the beat of your heart, hitting your drum, and playing your keys. I've found myself resorting to music at my lowest times in my early life to heal what wound had been made. From mistakes in my personal life especially the ones made in my previous relationship, I knew that finding

comfort in sound waves and frequencies would
rewire my thought processes.

Remember your value, your worth, and your
purpose. Don't let the heartbreak you face define
who you'll become.

Yellow

Yellow is the love you feel when you receive a hug

Yellow is the scent of sunflowers in flowing waves

Yellow tastes like the sweetest banana you'll ever eat

Yellow sounds like laughter on a warm sunny day

Yellow is the shining sun up in the sky

Colors.

Vibrant, Revolutionary.

Captivating, Overwhelming, Soothing.

A multiplicity of

Pigmentation.

Stacia Snowangel

The thought of losing you was ever so bitter,
With tears welling up and my heart tattered.
You smiled at me as I squirmed like a critter,
Little reminders of you in the house were
scattered.

When we first met you ran and fell on your face,
We held you oh so close.
The feeling of euphoria intertwined with grace,
As you walked proudly and wiggled your nose

You were always keen to squirrels on trees,
Yanking me around I'd fall on my behind,
Rock climbing in Maine and fuzzy bees,
I wish there was a chance I could rewind.

These memories are bittersweet and sting,
As I know your box is buried by your spot,
Your ashes remain where the lighthouse sings,
In Maine, you'll sleep, where the trees won't rot.

To My Beloved Grandfather

I'll miss the times we built,
Many puzzles together.
Your black coffee preference,
Will stick with me forever.

Watching tennis and cheering loudly,
We'd watch and laugh for hours.
As the backyard is filled with plants,
I find your smile among the flowers.

You loved to compliment meals,
The way your eyes lit like stars.
You'd often be proud to show me,
Your knowledge and collection of cars.

Novelty items and fun clothing to wear,
You'd rock them on every occasion.
Although sometimes you'd go extra,
You wore them out with persuasion.

Peapom would match your outfits,
You both shone so bright.
I always find your love in my mind,
The joy you had was quite a sight.

You gave me your pants,
As a precious hand down.
I'll wear your love forever,
I'll show it off around the town.

You made it to heaven,
To the party of eternity.
One day I'll join you,
To the place of harmony.

Puzzles and pictures,
On a solid wooden box.
Antiques and bridges,
With a hill and a fox.

One day I'll be old in age,
And my time will come.
But until then I'll live,
Out your legacy till I succumb.

I love you so much. Don't have too much fun
without me.